Sir Philip Francis

Answer of Philip Francis

To the Charge Brought Against Sir John Clavering, Colonel George

Monson, and Mr. Francis, at the Bar of the House of Commons, on the

fourth of February, 1788

Sir Philip Francis

Answer of Philip Francis
To the Charge Brought Against Sir John Clavering, Colonel George Monson, and Mr. Francis, at the Bar of the House of Commons, on the fourth of February, 1788

ISBN/EAN: 9783337139452

Printed in Europe, USA, Canada, Australia, Japan

Cover: Foto ©Suzi / pixelio.de

More available books at **www.hansebooks.com**

ANSWER

OF

PHILIP FRANCIS, Esq.

TO THE

C H A R G E

BROUGHT AGAINST

SIR JOHN CLAVERING,
COLONEL GEORGE MONSON,
AND MR. FRANCIS,

AT THE

BAR OF THE HOUSE OF COMMONS,

ON THE

FOURTH OF FEBRUARY, 1788;

BY

SIR ELIJAH IMPEY, KNIGHT.

———————

L O N D O N:

PRINTED BY J. JARVIS, WILD-COURT, LINCOLN'S-INN-
FIELDS.

MDCCLXXXVIII.

HOUSE OF COMMONS.

Wednesday, February 27, 1788.

" The House (according to Order) re-
" solved itself into a Committee of the
" whole House, to consider further of
" the several Articles of Charge of
" High Crimes and Misdemeanors
" against Sir *Elijah Impey*, Knight, late
" Chief Justice of the Supreme Court
" of Judicature at Fort William, in
" Bengal. *Right Honourable William*
" *Windham, Esq. in the Chair.*

MR. FRANCIS. I flattered myself, Sir,
that when the House thought proper to ex-
clude me from the Committee of Managers
appointed to conduct the impeachment of Mr.
Hastings, whether that resolution was meant
to be a discharge from a service, or a relief

B   from

from a duty, it would have this effect at all events—that, from thenceforward, I should be suffered to remain in a state of neutrality; and that, as I was deprived of the honour, I should be exempted from the cares and cenfures, to which the Managers of an Impeachment muft unavoidably fubmit. But much more had I reafon to expect that, after the public declaration which I made in Parliament two years ago*, *that I would never fit in judgement on Sir Elijah Impey; and that I would never give a judicial vote in any caufe, in which he might be a party, unlefs I could fafely give it for him;*—having publicly avowed that declaration in print, having fince repeatedly declared to my friends, particularly to the honourable Baronet † near me, that I would take no part in the profecution of Sir Elijah Impey, and having ftrictly adhered to the fpirit of thefe declarations, I fhould not be implicated, in any fhape, in the impeachment of that gentleman. Leaft of all did I expect, that I fhould be accufed by him of having borne teftimony to his good conduct, and compelled by him to anfwer, as a criminal,

* On the feventh of March, 1786.
† Sir Gilbert Elliot.

for

for declarations, which he tells you I have here-
tofore made in his favour. I do not mean to
deny his right of mixing accufation with defence, if to criminate others be in any degree
material, or even ufeful to his own exculpation.
In fome cafes undoubtedly, the weapons of attack are the beft, perhaps the only inftruments
of defence. Whether the ufe he has made of
thefe weapons, and the manner, in which he
has availed himfelf of his undifputed right on
this occafion, be perfectly prudent or not, can
only be determined by the event. All I contend for is, that *I*, in my turn, may be allowed
the fame latitude which *he* has taken, and
which *I* allow him. It is not my direct object
this day to criminate him, or any man ; but it
may be neceffary to my defence. It may be
unavoidable. Defence and accufation, in this
particular cafe, may be infeparable. If that
fhould happen, I defire it may be remembered,
that, befides the general right of attack which,
for myfelf, I admit to belong to him and to
every defendant, I appeal to the fpecific ufe,
which he has made of it, and follow the precedent, which he has himfelf fpecifically fet me.

On fome late occafions, my fituation, in this
Houfe, has been equally painful and invidious.

I have

I have been repeatedly marked as the perfonal object of debate,—the middle pafsive fubject between the action and reaction of the powers of the Houfe, between the hammer and the anvil. If any man thinks there is any thing delightful or agreeable in fuch a diftinction, I am fure his opinion is not founded on experience. I ftand here, now, defendant againft Sir Elijah Impey. In that character at leaft, I hope to be heard with patience and a liberal conftruction. I defire no more.

The charge produced by this gentleman againft Sir John Clavering, Colonel Monfon, and myfelf, as I underftood it, and as precifely as I have been able to collect it from my notes and memory, was, in real amount and fubftance, to this effect. It is his own fault if I do not ftate it correctly.

" That whereas we had, by fundry decla-
" rations and minutes, both before and after
" the event, expreffed, or ftrongly intimated
" our opinion, that the profecution, trial, and
" execution of Nundcomar, were founded on
" political motives, and purfued for the fole
" purpofe of faving Mr. Haftings from the
" effect of that man's evidence; no credit

" ought

" ought to be given to the fame, becaufe we
" had, in a few days after the execution, or-
" dered a paper, purporting to be a petition
" from Nundcomar againft the Judges, to
" be burnt, the entries of it to be expun-
" ged, and the tranflations to be deftroyed;
" and, becaufe I had, on that occafion, decla-
" red, that I confidered the infinuations con-
" tained in it as wholly unfupported, and of a
" libellous nature, and that to fend a copy of
" it to the Judges, would be giving it much
" more weight than it deferved."

If this be the charge, I admit the premifes,
and I deny the conclufion. If it be *not* the
charge, I fhall paufe for a moment, and wait
to be informed, *What is it?*—No man, I think,
will fay, that I have weakened or underftated
it. For myfelf, I declare that I am not able
to conceive, how it can be expreffed in ftrong-
er terms againft the parties accufed. If neverthelefs it fhould be contended, that the
terms I have made ufe of are loofe or defective, or that I have not done perfect juftice to
Sir Elijah Impey's meaning and intention, let
it be remembered, Sir, that he has not delivered his accufation in writing, as I had a
ftrict unqueftionable right to expect. Nothing

thing that may be urged to juftify his with-
holding the remainder of his defence, can be
applied to that part of it, in which others are
accufed. It might be very prudent in him ; it
might be effential to his fafety, not to put his
accufers in poffeffion of his defence. Be it fo.
In that refpect, he is at liberty to act as he
thinks proper ; though I believe his refufal to
produce his defence, in the only form in which
it could be fairly canvaffed, or even compared
with the written accufation, will not be received as a ftrong prefumptive proof even of
his own confidence in the merits of his caufe.
My demand is a demand of right. It is not
to oblige him to produce his defence, but to
produce his accufation. Before I proceed,
Sir, to the refutation of the charge, as I have
ftated it, the exactnefs of which, I perceive,
is not difputed, I muft call the attention of
the Committee to two preliminary confiderati-
ons, and requeft that gentlemen will carry
them in their minds during the fubfequent dif-
cuffion. They will throw a light on the general queftion, and, I believe, be found very
material to a thorough underftanding of the
whole tranfaction. I mean fimply to ftate them
now, and to referve the application of them for
another

another part of my defence.—The firft relates to the manner, in which the paper in queftion, came into Sir Elijah Impey's hands; the difficulties, which were to be furmounted before he could be in poffeffion of it; and the probable truth or falfehood of his affertion, that he never knew what the charges were, which Nundcomar had produced againft Mr. Haftings. I fhall recapitulate the facts to you briefly as they appear on the records, or as they have been ftated by Sir Elijah Impey.

The Rajah Nundcomar was executed on the 5th of Auguft, 1775. On the 14th, General Clavering brought the petition, which was afterwards burnt, before the Governor General and Council, in their fecret department. It was produced and read; but I conclude, that the tranflation, which the General brought with him, was not relied on, becaufe I find the next fecret confultation, of the 16th, begins with the following words* :—" The Perfian
" tranflator fends in a corrected tranflation of the
" petition of the late Maha Raja Nundcomar,
" delivered in by General Clavering."—Mr. Haftings immediately moved that, " as this

* Vide Bengal Appendix, page, 585.

" petition

" petition contained 'exprefsions reflecting
" upon the characters of the chief Juftice and
" Judges of the Supreme Court, a copy of it
" might be fent them." I objected to that
propofal, and moved, that orders fhould be
given to the Sheriff, to caufe the original to be
burned publicly by the hands of the common
hangman;—a fingular ftep, Sir, and on the
face of our proceedings utterly unaccountable.
Mr. Haftings repeatedly faid, that he did not
object to that motion; but he obferved that it
would not be effectual, " as the petition ftood
" on our own records, through which it
" would find its way to the Court of Direc-
" tors, to his Majefty's Minifters, and in all
" probability become public to the whole peo-
" ple of Britain." Admitting the force of the
obfervation, I propofed that *the entry of the
addrefs from Rajah Nundcomar fhould be expunged.*
On this motion, the *unanimous* refolution of the
board ftands in the following words—AGREED,
*that it be expunged accordingly; and that the tranf-
lations be deftroyed.* To this refolution Mr.
Haftings was a party, not only as a Member of
the Council, legally bound and concluded by
the fenfe of the majority, but by his own exprefs confent and agreement.

On

On the 28th of Auguft the Judges wrote to us in the following words * :

"A paper, containing a falfe, fcandalous,
" and malicious charge againft the Judges of
" the Supreme Court, produced at your
" Board, having been by you declared a libel,
" and ordered to be burnt by the hands of the
" common hangman, we return you our
" thanks for having fhewn fo due a fenfe of
" this outrage to public juftice ; but, as we
" muft be interefted as well in the Minutes
" introducing and condemning the paper, as
" in the paper itfelf, we find ourfelves obliged
" to defire that you will furnifh us with a co-
" py of the libel, and of fuch Minutes, which
" relate to it, as ftand on your confultations,
" and muft therefore be conveyed to England,
" that we may judge whether they contain any
" matters NECESSARY FOR US TO TAKE NO-
" TICE OF."

In our reply, dated 11th September, we faid†,
" We fhall be much obliged to you, if you
" will be pleafed to acquaint us, from whom
" you received the imperfect information

* Page 586.   † Page 589.

C   " which

" which appears to have been conveyed to
" you, on this and other occafions, of the
" proceedings of this Board in our fecret de-
" partment; fuch communications cannot re-
" gularly be made to you but by the authority
" of the Board; nor can they be obtained
" without a breach of truft in fome of our
" officers, which we are perfuaded you would
" not encourage.

" We do not think ourfelves at liberty to
" communicate to you the Minutes, which
" may have paffed on the prefent fubject, as
" fuch Minutes are drawn up folely for the
" information of our fuperiors. With refpect
" to the libel, it is not poffible for us to fur-
" nifh you with a copy of that paper, having
" ordered the original and tranflations to be
" deftroyed, *and no copy to be kept of either.*" —
This letter, you will obferve, was figned by
Mr. Haftings, who knew that he, alone, had
given the information,—who had agreed to
the refolution of the Board, that the original
paper and tranflations fhould be deftroyed, and
that no copy fhould be kept of either;—who
neverthelefs kept a copy of the tranflation,
(which he muft have obtained from the Perfian
tranflator, by a breach of duty in that officer) who
knew

knew that he had given, or intended to give a copy of that tranflation to Sir Elijah Impey; and who not only did fo, but, as it now appears, altered the tranflation, made by the proper officer of government, in many places, with his own hand; and it is by this laft extraordinary circumftance that Sir Elijah Impey proves the authenticity of the paper, which he produces in his defence, namely, that it is altered, corrected, and interlined in Mr. Haftings's hand-writing. Mr. Haftings, I know, did not agree to the letter, though he figned it; his diffent is recorded in the following words:

" I difapprove of the draught, becaufe I " do not think the information imperfect, " which was received by the Judges; becaufe " it appears to me an inconfiftency to fpeak of " a paper, which was expunged from the re-" cords, and ordered to be publicly burnt by " the common hangman, as a fecret of ftate, " which it was a breach of truft to divulge; " and becaufe the letter is written *in a ftrain of* *" infinuation*, equally unbecoming the dignity " of the Board, and deficient in the refpect, " which is due to the Judges of the Court, to " whom it is addreffed."

This

This diffent, you fee, is fupported by every
argument he could think of, except the true
one. He does not tell us, that he himfelf had
given the information; that he himfelf had
kept a copy of the tranflation; that he himfelf
had corrected, and given it to Sir Elijah Impey.
Had he affigned the true reafon for his diffent,
we muft have given a very different anfwer to
the Judges. It would have been impoffible
even for *us* to fign fuch a letter as that, which
we all figned; much lefs could we have defired,
or expected Mr. Haftings to put his name to
it. It may be faid perhaps, that he was bound
by a provifion in the Act of Parliament, and
by the forms of the Council, to fign a letter refolved on by the majority, even againft his opinion. That he was legally fo bound and concluded, I admit; but that in fact he fubmit-
ted to the law, I deny. On other occafions it
appears that he did not hold himfelf bound, by
any obligation whatever, legal or formal, to
fign a letter, of which he difapproved *.

Tho

* On the 16th of the preceding June, 1775, the
majority refolved on a letter to the Judges, to which Mr.
Haftings did not agree. Did he fign it with a diffent?
No—

The ftudied terms of evafion, in which Sir Elijah Impey declined anfwering our requifition, deferve your attention, but they require no comment. He fays*, " Our letter men-
" tions no information we had received from
" your Board ; we cannot fee what reafon you
" have to fuppofe we have received any. We
" fhall, at all times, be ready to give you
" any information and affiftance in our power,
" in forwarding the public bufinefs, but muft
" decline making a precedent of fubmitting to
" anfwer queftions, which we think not intend-
" ed for the benefit of the fervice, and which
" you have neither grounds nor right to put
" to us."

(Signed)   " E. IMPEY,
                  " JOHN HYDE."

No—the records fays, [page 575] " The Governor Gene-
" ral, and Mr. Barwell, difapproving of this reply, decline
" affixing their names to it, for which they will affign their
" reafons in a Minute." On the 20th of June they refufed
to fign another letter to the Judges, which was accordingly fent without their fignature ; and Mr. Haftings faid
he thought himfelf juftified in that refufal, *both by the
let ter of the law, and the fpirit of the Company's orders.*
[page 607]

* Page 590.

Sir

Sir Elijah Impey tells you, on another occafion, and to ferve another material purpofe,
that he knew nothing of the contents of the
charges of Nundcomar againft Mr. Haftings.
His words, as I wrote them down upon the
inftant, were; " I aver, that I did not know
" what they were. How fhould I? They
" were produced before a fecret Council, and
" examined by a fecret Committee, of which
" all the members, their clerks and fecreta-
" ries, were *fworn to fecrecy*."—Now, Sir, admitting it to be poffible, that Sir Elijah Impey
might not know, from public report, the fpecific fums ftated, or the particular facts and
circumftances charged by Nundcomar againft
Mr. Haftings, that admiffion will not avail
him. You are called upon to believe, that Sir
Elijah Impey, living in the clofeft connection
and intimacy with Mr. Haftings, did not know
what was known to every man in Calcutta;
what was the univerfal fubject of converfation there for many months together, namely,
that Nundcomar had accufed Mr. Haftings of
venality and corruption in his office. He did
not know that this charge was laid before the
Council on the 11th of March; that Nundcomar had been examined before the Council;

that

that, on the 20th of April, Nundcomar was summoned to appear before all the Judges, to answer to a charge of a conspiracy against Mr. Hastings; and that, having been acquitted and difmissed on that examination, he was, on the 6th of May, arrested, and committed to the common jail, by a warrant signed by two of the Judges, upon a charge of forgery. The facts at least were too public and too notorious not to be known to him. But we are to believe that, knowing such facts, it never once occurred to him, that there could be any relation between the first and all that followed it. Being ignorant, as he assures you, of the particulars of the charge against Mr. Hastings, he never once suspected that that act of Nundcomar could have been the motive of those subsequent measures, which were taken to destroy him. Any other man, I think, would have combined the circumstances. In any other human mind, they must have excited some degree of suspicion. My Honourable Friend, I doubt not, will be able to satisfy this House, in proper time, that the general fact, namely, that Nundcomar had brought a criminal charge against Mr. Hasting., and even the special nature of that charge, were

judicially

judicially known to Sir Elijah Impey long before the execution. What I contend for, and
infift upon now, is, that it is a thing utterly
incredible; that it is a belief, to which no human credulity can extend, that Mr. Haftings,
who, in the face of the moft facred obligation and engagement, thought himfelf at liberty to communicate to Sir Elijah Impey the
petition of Nundcomar, to give him a corrected
tranflation of it, and to furnifh him, as I fhall
prove he did, with copies of our Minutes,
directly arraigning the conduct of Sir Elijah
Impey in the trial and execution of Nundcomar, fhould not have imparted to him the
charges preferred againft himfelf by Nundcomar, which, though entered in the fecret department, were neither of a fecret nature in
themfelves, nor in fact a fecret to any man in
Calcutta.

The fecond preliminary obfervation, which I
wifh to imprefs on the minds of the Committee, regards the diftinction, which Sir Elijah
Impey carefully makes, and ftrenuoufly infifts
on, between the paper itfelf, and our *Minutes,*
upon the fubject ;—the firft he faw ; the fecond
he never faw, till very lately, when he obtained a copy of them from the India Houfe.

It

It is indeed not only material, but effential to his defence, that he fhould perfuade you of the truth of this laft affertion. He well knew, though you are not aware of it, that, if he admitted that he had feen our Minutes of the 16th of Auguft 1775, at any time before January 1776, he muft have convicted himfelf of the groffeft falfehood and contradiction. I fhall fpeak to that point prefently. But it feems that he not only did not fee them in the year 1775, but that he never faw them at all, *till very lately*. Now, Sir, I beg leave in the firft place to obferve, that the Minutes in queftion, on the prefent production of which he profeffes to place fo much reliance, have not been concealed from the world; have not been buried in obfcurity. The books, now before me, (called the Bengal Narrative and Appendix) muft have been printed by the Court of Directors in the year 1776, or 1777; I prefume fo, becaufe I had a copy of them, long before I left Bengal, in the courfe of the year 1778, if not fooner. There were other copies in Calcutta. They were read with avidity by every man in the fettlement, who could procure a fight of them. They contain not only our Minutes, but great

D   part

part of our proceedings, and all our corref-
pondence with Sir Elijah Impey, on the fubject of Nundcomar. To all other men, the
contents muft have been an object of curiofity
at leaft. I know they were fo. To *him*, in particular, they were in the higheft degree in-
terefting and important. Yet the learned gentleman never faw them in Bengal ; thefe books
it feems, *never* fell into his hands ! nay, you
are to be believe that, among the number of
perfons, by whom they were unqueftionably
perufed, he had no acquaintance, who might
have told him that fuch a compilation, pub-
liſhed by authority, and in which his name
and conduct were fo often mentioned, exifted
in Calcutta. He had no friend or well-wiſher,
among that number, who might have waited
on him, as foon as he had read our Minutes,
to congratulate him on the teftimony given,
as you are told, by his enemies or opponents,
in favour of his integrity, and to recommend
thofe paffages at leaft to his immediate pe-
rufal. Believe it if you will ; believe it if you
can. Perhaps you may think that, having
gone fo far, you have done enough, and that
Sir Elijah Impey has no farther demand
on your credulity. That learned gentle-

man

man is not fo eafily fatisfied. It feems, Sir,
he knew the facts ; he knew that we had ordered a libel on the Supreme Court of Judicature to be burned, and that it was burned ;
he had feen the paper itfelf, and was in poffeffion of a copy of it, given him by Mr. Haftings ; but he had never, *never* feen the Minutes that related to it ! Now, Sir, it is of
itfelf an extraordinary circumftance, that Mr.
Haftings, who thought himfelf at liberty to
give him the paper, in violation, as I think, of
the laws of the Council, and of his own perfonal agreement, fhould not have communicated to him thofe Minutes, which make an
effential part of the tranfaction, and which, if
they were then fuppofed to mean what he tells
you they fo clearly exprefs, were not only innocent of all offence to the Judges, but conveyed a pofitive approbation of their conduct.
Why fhould Mr. Haftings make fo partial a
communication of our proceedings to Sir Elijah Impey ?—Why fhould the Governor General with-hold from the Chief Juftice the fair
and reafonable fatisfaction of knowing that we,
his enemies, had borne teftimony to the rectitude of his conduct, and vindicated his character from every afperfion, which might have

been

been, or could be thrown upon it. I defy any man to state a principle of action that will justify Mr. Haftings in doing the first, and not doing the second ; or a rational motive of any kind, to make it probable in fact, that he did the one and not the other. The affertion is, that Mr. Haftings did not communicate our Minutes on this occasion to Sir Elijah Impey. Why not ?—perhaps he thought it unfair;—perhaps he thought it would have been a breach of truft and honour to his colleagues.—Perhaps he made a diftinction between the paper itfelf, which, as he fays, *having been ordered to be publickly burnt, could be no fecret of ftate**, and the Minutes of the Council, given in fecret debate and recorded for the fole information of the Court of Directors. —In general, there might have been fomething, though in this cafe there would have been nothing in the diftinction;—but in fact, did he make the diftinction? I appeal to Sir Elijah Impey, and fhall leave it to him to anfwer the queftion. In his letter of the 20th of January 1776, in four or five months after the tranfaction of which we are fpeaking, he tells the Secretary of State, " The Governor General has, within

* Page 589.

" thefe

" thefe few days, communicated to me feveral
" Minutes, figned by General Clavering, Colo-
" nel Monfon, and Mr. Francis ; they are feve-
" rally fraught with direct charges, or plain
" infinuations againft the characters of the
" Judges, and the conduct of the Court of
" Judicature. Some feem more particularly
" levelled at *me*." You have it then from unqueftionable authority, that Mr. Haftings did
communicate our Minutes to Sir Elijah Impey :
—Minutes fraught with direct charges againft
him :—Minutes, which, as he, *Impey*, fays,
*were intended to be kept fecret ; but the Governor
General had at laft thought, that they ought in juftice to be communicated to him.*—Did he fo ? Then
where was the juftice of Mr. Haftings, when
he communicated to his learned friend thofe
fecret Minutes of ours, which were fraught
with charges againft him, and did not communicate to him thofe other Minutes, in which,
as this learned gentleman tells you, we had expreffed a direct, unequivocal approbation of
his conduct ? was it a fair and honourable proceeding to his colleagues ? would it have been
common juftice even to his enemies, to impart
the one, and not the other, to the perfon, who
was the fubject of both ; to impart to Sir Elijah
Impey

Impey every thing that was likely to inflame him againft us, and to withhold from his knowledge what might have operated in his mind, as an antidote againft that poifon ; namely, the ftrong declarations which we are ftated to have made in his favour ? was it juft to Sir E. I. to difcover to him the charges, which we had written home againft him, and not to furnifh him with that clear, complete, and irrefiftible anfwer, which had efcaped or been extorted from us, by which the charges might not only have been refuted, but muft have been annihilated ; I mean the direct teftimony and confeffion of his accufers ? For my part, Sir, I acquit Mr. Haftings of acting fo unjuftly to all parties ; to his friend, as well as to his foes. I acquit him of it, becaufe I am not able to conceive a reafon, good or bad, why he fhould act in a manner at once fo unfair to his colleagues, and fo injurious to his friend. I have no doubt that he communicated *all* our Minutes to Sir Elijah Impey. In proper time, I fhall fhew you, for what reafon the contrary is maintained by this learned gentleman. On this part of the fubject, I fhall trouble you with only one obfervation more.— The Judges, in their letter of the 28th of Auguft

guft 1775, tranfmitted to us certain petitions*,
which had been addreffed to them, in order that
they might ftafd recorded † on our confultations; " which," they fay, " we think pecu-
" liarly proper at this time; as, by promul-
" gating the univerfal fenfe of this fettlement,
" in relation to our conduct, they are a di-
" rect and public refutation of the libel, and
" corroborate fuch of your Minutes, as tend
" to vindicate our reputations."—Now, Sir,
if he had not feen our fecret confultations of
the 16th of Auguft, how came he to know,
that thofe or any other Minutes exifted? How
could he make the diftinction hetweeñ fuch as
did and fuch as did not tend to vindicate his
reputation? Mine was the only Minute of the .
three, to which, by any poffible conftruction,
that tendency could be imputed. Is it not
evident from this paffage alone, that he had a
copy of the confultation before him ; or, what

* Sir Elijah Impey has lived to alter his opinion of
Petitions. In his letter to Lord Weymouth, of the 2nd
of March, 1780, he fays, " the only manner, in which
" the obtaining Petitions here differs from the modes
" practifed by factions in Englind, is—there they are
" folicited, and got by influence—here they are com-
" manded."

* Page 586.

is

is in effect the fame, that the fubftance of our
different Minutes had been diftinctly ftated
to him.—From all the premifes, taken together, I . draw this immediate inference of fact
which, as I conceive, it is impoffible for the
human mind to refift, and which, for other
reafons, I know to be true, namely that, while
he pretended *to be fcrupuloufly neuter in the difputes, which agitated the Council,* he was fecretly
leagued in early connexion, in clofe communication, in deep alliance and confederacy
with Mr. Haftings. In what fenfe that fact is
material to my defence, and in what manner I
mean to apply it, will foon appear.

I muft now requeft the Committee to obferve, that there are two parties concerned in
the accufation brought againft us by Sir Elijah
Impey;—one, the then majority of the Council collectively, viz. General Clavering, Colonel Monfon, and myfelf;—the other, Sir John
Clavering alone. Our caufes are diftinct, and
muft be feparately confidered and defended.
With refpect to the former of thefe parties, I
have already ftated to you the recorded facts
of the tranfaction, in the order in which they
happened. I am now to ftate the reafons of

our

our conduct; I mean, not only our avowed,
but our reserved reasons for acting as we did.

In reply to the Governor's motion, I said *
that " I thought our sending a copy of the
" Raja Nundcomar's address to our Board, to
" the Chief Justice and the Judges, would be
" giving it much more weight than it deserv-
" ed; and that I confidered the infinuations,
" contained in it, againft them, as wholly un-
" fupported, and of a libellous nature." In the
whole of that opinion Colonel Monfon agreed;
but he added, " that if the Board fhould com-
" municate the paper to the Judges, he thought
" *they* (the Members of the Board) might be
" liable to a profecution for a libel." General
Clavering difapproved of the propofition, " be-
" caufe he thought it might make the Mem-
" bers of the Board, who fent it, liable to a
" profecution." The Governor General and
Council having unanimoufly agreed that the
Perfian paper fhould be publicly deftroyed, I
concluded the debate with another motion, in
the following words* :—" By the fame channel
" through which the Court of Directors, and
" his Majefty's Minifters, and the nation,
" might be informed of the contents of the pa-

* Page 585.   † Page 586.

E   " per

" per in queſtion, they muſt alſo be informed
" of the reception it had met with, and the
" ſentence paſſed upon it at this Board. I
" therefore hope that its being deſtroyed in the
" manner propoſed, will be ſufficient to clear
" the character of the Judges, *ſo far as they ap-*
" *pear to be attacked in that paper*; and to pre-
" vent any poſſibility of the imputations, indi-
" rectly thrown on the Judges, from extend-
" ing beyond this Board, I move that the en-
" try of the addreſs from Rajah Nundcomar,
" entered on our proceedings of Monday laſt,
" be expunged."

Before I offer any obſervation on the true
intent and meaning of theſe Minutes, allow me
to read to you a few ſhort paſſages out of
other Minutes of ours, written both before and
after the execution of Nundcomar, in which
our opinion of the real principle and purpoſe
of that proceeding is very ſtrongly and very
explicitly declared.

" *Minute of Mr.* FRANCIS.

April 24, 1775*.
" I beg leave to obſerve, that a proſecution
" for a conſpiracy is now inſtituted, or is in-

* Page 550.

" tended

" tended to be inftituted, againft Maha Rajah
" Nundcomar and others, the tendency of
" which feems to me to be to prevent or deter
" him from proceeding in making good thofe
" difcoveries, which he has laid before the
" Board. I cannot but think that the Eaft
" India Company, and confequently this
" Board, have a very great concern in every
" ftep taken in that profecution, whether it
" be actually begun, or intended."

Minute of GENERAL CLAVERING.

8*th May,* 1775*.

" In reply to what the Governor General
" has juft faid, I conceive that the protection
" of the inhabitants of Bengal is immediately
" trufted to our care, and that it properly be-
" longs to us to reprefent to the Judges fuch
" matters as may appear to us, wherein they
" have acted improperly, either wilfully or
" ignorantly. In the prefent inftance, they
" probably are ignorant, how much a clofe
" confinement may endanger the life of this
" man, which is of fo much importance to
" the public, for proving an accufation, which
" he has made of cruality in the Governor Ge-
" neral."

* Page 558.

E 2   *Extract*

Extract of a Minute of CLAVERING, MONSON, *and* FRANCIS.

Sept. 15, 1775.

" After the death of Nundcomar, the Go-
" vernor, we believe, is well affured that no
" man, who regards his fafety, will venture to
" ftand forth as his accufer.

" On a fubject of this delicate nature, it be-
" comes us to leave every honeft man to his
" own reflexions. It ought to be made known
" however to the Englifh nation, that the for-
" gery, of which the Raja was accufed, muft
" have been committed feveral years ago; that
" in the interim he had been protected and
" employed by Mr. Haftings; that his fon was
" appointed to one of the firft offices in the
" Nabob's houfehold, with a falary of one lack
" of rupees; that the accufation, which ended
" in his deftruction, was not produced till he
" came forward, and brought a fpecific charge
" againft the Governor General of corruption
" in his office."

Ditto of ditto.

" We agree with Mr. Haftings, that not
" only he himfelf, but many other perfons in

" this

" this fettlement, have reafon to thank God,
" as he expreffes it, for the inftitution of this
" Court."

Ditto, dated Nov. 21, 1775.

" It feems probable, fuch embezzlements
" may have been univerfally practifed. In the
" prefent circumftances, it will be difficult, if
" not impracticable, to obtain direct proof of
" the facts. The terror, impreffed on the minds
" of the natives by the execution of Maha
" Rajah Nundcomar, is not to be effaced;
" for, though he fuffered for the crime of
" forgery, yet the natives conceive he was ex-
" ecuted for having dared to prefer complaints
" againft the Governor General.

" This idea, however deftitute of founda-
" tion, is prevalent among the natives, and
" will naturally deter them from making dif-
" coveries, which may be attended with the
" fame fatal confequences to themfelves.

" Punifhment is ufually intended as an ex-
" ample, to prevent the commiffion of crimes;
" in this inftance, we fear, it has ferved to
" prevent the difcovery of them."

Ditto, March 21, 1776.

" Some of the facts, with which he (Mr.
" Haftings) has been perfonally charged, have
" been proved. The prefumptive evidence,
" in fupport of the reft, will, we apprehend,
" lofe none of its force, by the precipitate re-
" moval of Maha Rajah Nundcomar."

Now, Sir, if it be true that there is a mani-
feft inconfiftency, a palpable contradiction between thefe declarations, and our intermediate
proceedings on the 16th Auguft, 1775, I have
brought that inconfiftency and contradiction
plainly and diftinctly into your view. I am
fure I can fatisfy the Committee that it does not
exift. In the firft place, you will allow me to
fay that, fetting afide all confideration of moral character, and claiming nothing in favour
of General Clavering, Colonel Monfon, and
myfelf, but that we fhall not be taken for
idiots, it is not very likely that, having repeatedly charged the profecution and execution of Nundcomar againft Sir Elijah Impey,
as a political meafure of the moft atrocious
kind; having fo often recorded that opinion
on the proceedings of the Council, we fhould
almoft at the fame moment, voluntarily, and
                                        without

without any apparent reafon, deliberately con-
tradict ourfelves, and record our own condem-
nation on the face of our proceedings. Is it a
thing to be believed, that having advanced
fuch a charge, we fhould fo lightly abandon it,
and that, having abandoned, we fhould re-
fume and re-affert it, without once attempting
to reconcile or explain the inconfiftency of our
conduct, if the idea of that contradiction, which
is now urged and infifted on, had ever occurred
to us? Is it likely that, while we were con-
tending with Mr. Haftings for the good opinion of the Court of Directors, we fhould have
placed ourfelves before them in a point of
view, which muft have utterly annihilated
their confidence in us?—Sir, I affirm that, in
fact, we did no fuch thing. The terms of
my opinion of the contents of the paper,
which I propofed fhould be deftroyed, are, I
fee, particularly relied on. I defire they may
be ftrictly examined. I faid that to fend
to the Judges a copy of Nundcomar's petition,
would be giving it much more weight than
it deferved; that I confidered the infinuations
contained in it againft them as wholly unfupported, and of a libellous nature. I thought
and faid fo then. I think and fay fo ftill, in
the

the extent and manner in which they were
ftated in that paper. The perfon, in whofe
name it appeared, was dead. He had, whether juftly or unjuftly, legally or illegally,
, been convicted of a crime, and had fuffered
an ignominious death. Even if he had been
refpited after conviction, his evidence would
have been ufelefs, for his credit was gone. A
petition from fuch a perfon, accufing his
Judges, could have no fort of weight. It
came before us without a refponfible accufer,
without a proof, or evidence of any kind; I
therefore faid it was *wholly unfupported*. No
man, I prefume, will deny that it was in ftrict-
nefs of *a libellous nature*. I afferted then, as I
affert now, that it was a libel on the whole
Court of Juftice, in the ftrict and proper fenfe
of the word. The dreadful charge contained
in it, included *all* the Judges, concerning two
of whom (Sir Robert Chambers and Mr. Hyde)
we never had a fufpicion of the motives, which
we attributed to Sir Elijah Impey, though I
am far from acquitting them of all blame.
Concerning another of the Judges, the late Mr.
Lemaiftre, though we faw him united in the
clofeft intimacy with the Chief Juftice, and
ready to fupport his opinions on all occafions,

2   with

with a degree of zeal and paffion which, however fincere, was not to be excufed, yet in
that, which conftitutes the deadly guilt of the
tranfaction, we never fufpected him to be concerned;—in a confederacy I mean with Sir Elijah Impey to take off Nundcomar, in order to
fave Mr. Haftings from the effect of that man's
evidence. We were bound therefore to treat
the petition as an indifcriminate libel againft a
whole Court of Juftice. Is there any thing in
that refolution, or in the terms of my opinion, on which it was founded, that under
any, I will not fay fair and liberal, but under
the moft rigorous conftruction, can be underftood to exprefs or fignify that we thought the
paper *falfe*, as well as libellous of all the
Judges? This is no new diftinction, fet up by
me to ferve the prefent purpofe. It is no after thought, no *ex poft faɛo* vindication of my
conduct. I can prove to the Committee, that
I always made the fame diftinction between an
accufation and a libel. When Mr. Haftings
accufed me perfonally, about three months before, of prefenting a libel againft him to the
Board, my anfwer to him ftands recorded in
the following words:

F

Extract

Extract of a Minute of Mr. FRANCIS.

March 21, 1775.

" The Governor General, who had long ex-
" pected the appearance of fuch a letter, and
" was apprifed of the contents of it, made no
" objection, however, to its being received
" and read at the Board. When the man,
" who advances a fpecific charge, declares
" himfelf ready to come forward and fupport
" it, and to hazard the confequences of fail-
" ing in his proofs, it may ftill indeed be pre-
" fumed that the charge is falfe; but it does
" not partake of the nature of a libel. A li-
" beller advances charges, which he does not
" intend, or is unable to make good. When
" called upon to appear and produce his evi-
" dence, he fhelters himfelf, fometimes in the
" obfcurity, fometimes in the fuperiority of
" his fituation, and leaves the accufation with-
" out an accufer, to operate as far as it can,
" in the opinions of men, againft the honour
" and reputation of the party accufed. Rajah
" Nundcomar is not an obfcure perfon in this
" country, nor does he in this inftance act the
" part of a libeller. He is himfelf of very
" high rank; he publickly accufes the Gover-

2   " nor

" nor General of misconduct in his office, and
" desires to be heard in person in support of
" his charge."

This is my defence against the charge, as it
affects us collectively on the face of our proceedings; and I willingly submit to your judgment, whether the avowed ostensible reasons,
publicly assigned by me, be not sufficient to
account for my public official conduct on the
occasion, and to acquit me of the present
charge of contradiction. But had I no other
motives for what I did, beyond those which I
have assigned? Undoubtedly I had, and I am
ready to declare them. Addressing you, as I
do, under an honourable and moral obligation,
as powerful and coercive as any, that law or
religion can impose upon the human mind, I
should hold myself a perjured man, if called
upon, as in effect I am, for the whole truth, I
reserved any part of it from your knowledge.
My secret predominant motive for proposing   V
to destroy the original paper produced by General Clavering, was to save *him*, and *him* alone,
from the danger, to which he had exposed him-
self by that rash inconsiderate action.   Yet   /
the step I took was not immediately taken on

F 2   my

my own fuggeftion. As foon as Mr, Haftings
propofed that a copy of the paper fhould be
fent to the Judges,—a ftep fufpicious on the
face of it, and by which it was impoffible any
good purpofe could be anfwered,—Colonel
Monfon ftarted at it, and defired me to go
with him into another room. Poffibly Mr.
Barwell may recolleᶜt the circumftance. He
then faid, " I fuppofe you fee what the
" Governor means. If the Judges get pof-
" feffion of the paper, Clavering may be
" ruined by it." My anfwer was, " Why,
" what can they do to him?" To that he
replied, " I know not what they can do;
" but, fince they have dipped their hands in
" blood, what is there they will not do?"—
He then defired me to move that the original
paper fhould be deftroyed by the hands of the
common hangman. This fhort converfation
paffed very nearly, I firmly believe, if not
precifely, in the terms in which I have related
it. It is not poffible I fhould ever forget or
miftake the fubftance of it. If I am charged
with having aᶜted a feeble, pufillanimous part,
let it be remembered that my fears, whether
well or ill founded, were not for myfelf; that
the danger, whether real or imaginary, could
no

no way extend to *me*. To fear nothing when we ourselves are in no danger, is not an unqueftionable proof of refolution;—much lefs is it a proof of timidity to fear every thing for the fafety of a friend. It was my opinion, however, and is fo at this hour, that the danger to General Clavering was real and ferious. The author of the libel was dead. General Clavering had made himfelf the publifher, and put himfelf into the power of his enemies. I cannot bring before you in evidence the ftate of the fettlement at that time; the great power that was confederated againft us, and the univerfal combination of all ranks of Europeans to fupport that power in all its operations. We were fent out by Parliament to enquire into and to reform abufes. The firft difcoveries, that came before us, gave a general alarm. The caufe of Mr. Haftings was made and declared to be the common caufe and intereft of all the Company's fervants. We, on the contrary, were confidered as their common enemy, and were at once the object of their jealoufy, their fear, and deteftation. With a very few exceptions, we three in effect ftood alone againft the combined power of two Members of the Council, one of whom was the Governor General;

againft

againſt the Supreme Court of Judicature, againſt the Board of Trade, and againſt the united animoſity and clamour of the whole ſettlement. If, in that ſtate and temper of the times, General Clavering had been indicted for a libel on the Supreme Court, whoſe powers were in effect, to us, undeſined, unlimited, and ſubject to nocontroul*, I cannot poſitively affirm what would have been the conſequence; but I am poſitively ſure, that no efforts would have been ſpared, no methods unattempted to haraſs and diſtreſs him, and, if poſſible, accompliſh his ruin. This I declare upon my honour, and am ready to declare upon my oath, was *my* motive, as I am convinced it was that of Colonel Monſon, for inſiſting that the original paper ſhould be deſtroyed. I do not expect, that the force of this motive ſhould be felt in this place and at the preſent hour, as it was by *us*, upon the ſpot, and in the moment of ac-

---

* Sir Elijah Impey, in his letter of the 15th of May 1775, (Page 563.) ſays, " The bounds, between the " authority of the Supreme Court and the Council, are " of too delicate a nature to be diſcuſſed, without there " ſhould be, which I truſt there never will be, an abſo- " lute neceſſity to determine them."

tion.

tion. The period is too remote. The scene is too diftant. The inftant impreffion upon our minds cannot eafily be communicated to yours. We knew we were furrounded by the fnares of the law. We had no legal learning. We had no legal advice. You may fpeculate coolly and wifely upon our conduct; but you will not determine equitably, if you do not endeavour to place yourfelves exactly in our fituation. At all events, whether we did right or wrong, we certainly did not do that of which we are accufed. We never faid, that the contents of Nundcomar's petition were not true. As Mr. Haftings entirely agreed with us in every thing we did, I never had a doubt that the tranflation was deftroyed, until Sir Elijah Impey produced a copy of it at the bar of this Houfe. Of the authenticity of this tranflation, you have no other evidence but that, which confeffes it was obtained by means the moft unjuftifiable, by means, which prove, what we always fufpected, that we were betrayed, by one of our own Board, to Sir Elijah Impey, and by means, which prove to demonftration the collufion and confederacy, that fubfifted from the firft between Sir Elijah Impey and Mr. Haftings. The exiftence of

that

that well-grounded fufpicion is material to our defence.

I am now to reply to that part of Sir Elijah Impey's accufation, which exclufively affects General Clavering. On my own account perfonally, I have no manner of concern in it. I am here the uninftructed advocate, the feeble defendant of an honourable friend, who is now no more. In *his* name, and for his caufe, I claim and expect that indulgence, that favour and protection, which he, I am fure, would never have folicited for himfelf, but which is admitted to be due, and which this Houfe, in fact, has liberally diftributed to other defendants. The learned gentleman himfelf, when he appeared at your bar, was received there, as he ought to be, with favour and indulgence. He was received there, with what I believe is not quite fo common, though perhaps equally proper, with diftinguifhed marks of protection. But if indulgence, if favour and protection are due to a perfon, who is prefent to defend himfelf, who is himfelf a man of great learning and experience, and who can at any time collect and command the united learning of his profeffion, and fummon it to his affiftance : how much more are they due to a man

of

of great character, who is not here to plead his own caufe; who is not only abfent, but dead, and who died in the fervice of his country. Not, indeed, in the field of battle, where his gallant mind would have led him, but in a vile, vexatious conteft with men;—I will not attempt to qualify them;—General Clavering thought himfelf degraded by a conteft with fuch men.

In this tranfaction, I cannot undertake to an-fwer for all the motions of his conduct. I think I can for fome of them. But affuredly, Sir, I fhall not attempt to explain what I never underftood; that is, with what inten-tion, and for what poffible purpofe, he brought the paper before the Board. Neither is that queftion material at prefent. The queftionable words in his Minute of the 14th of Auguft, 1775, when he produced the Petition of Nundcomar, are thefe : " As I imagined " that the Paper might contain fome requeft " that I fhould take fome fteps to intercede " for him, and being refolved not to make any " applications whatever in his favour, I left " the Paper on my table till the 6th, which " was the day after his execution, when I " ordered it to be tranflated by my interpre- " ter."—On this proceeding, the queftion is

too

too obvious not to occur inftantly to every man who hears me, *why had he refolved not to make any application whatever in favour of Nundcomar?*

In attempting to account for an act done by another, fo many years ago, and to verify the motives of the perfon who did it ; you will not expect that the evidence fhould amount to demonftration. The beft that I can offer you, and the utmoft the cafe will admit of, is ftrong probability and fair con-jecture. The peculiar character and known principles of General Clavering muft be taken into the account. Remember that you áre trying a caufe of honour in a Court of Honour, in the *forum confcientiæ*, which exifts in the heart of every honourable man, not in a Court of Law. You cannot fairly pronounce upon the man, without knowing and confidering the general principles of his life. Now, Sir, I affirm of General Clavering, what I believe will not be difputed by any perfon who knew him, that his moral mind and character were ftrictly and feverely upright; that he determined every queftion that came before him with ri-gid juftice ; that his delicacy, in every thing that appeared to him to touch his honour, was more than fcrupulous, and bordered, if pof-

fible

fible, upon excefs. I have fometimes told him fo, when I have feen him refufe little complimentary prefents of fruit, or flowers, fent to his family, and order them to be returned.—He was a man very tender of public reputation; very fearful of reproach; and particularly fearful of the imputation of fupporting and encouraging the accufer of Mr. Haftings. With thefe principles, he might poffibly think that it did not become him to intercede for a man found guilty of a capital offence. But it is much more probable, and more material to his prefent vindication, that he was well convinced his interceffion would do mifchief inftead of good, and would rather haften than retard the execution of Nundcomar. Mr. Farrer tells you in his evidence*, that when he propofed to the General to receive and tranfmit to the Judges, a Petition of Nundcomar addreffed to the Governor General and Council, his anfwer ended with thefe words, " *nor indeed did he think it would do any* " *good.*" That he had folid and fufficient reafon for entertaining that opinion, I believe I can demonftrate. Many gentlemen, I dare fay, who heard Sir Elijah Impey's fugitive de-

* Page 22.

fence

fence at the Bar, went away with an impreffion, that General Clavering, Colonel Monfon and I, never took any formal fteps in favour
of Nundcomar; and that if we had interceded
for him, it might probably have faved his
life. Whether the Judges would or would
not have yielded to our interceffion, is a queftion, which no human tribunal can decide.
You may form a judgment of it, however,
by obferving how the Court acted, when we
really did intercede with them in favour of
Nundcomar, in inftances of no importance to
the real purpofes of juftice, though very important to the unfortunate man himfelf. I
fhall ftate the facts I allude to, in the terms in
which they are recorded.

On the 8th of May, 1775,* a Petition was
received from Rajah Nundcomar to the Governor General and Council, which, after
ftating many other particulars, very deferving of the attention of the Houfe of Commons, concludes with the following words,—
" The Honourable Prefident, I am well af-
" fured, is fully fenfible of the facts I allude
" to;—It may be requifite to explain to the
" reft of the Honourable Members of the

* Page 552.

" Board,

" Board, that the inftitutions of our religion
" ftrictly enjoin a number of ablutions, pray-
" ers, and other ceremonies to be performed
" by the fect of Bramins, before they can
" take any kind of food. Nothing of this
" can be performed in the place where I now
" am ; and, could even thefe obftacles be
" furmounted, the place itfelf, as being in-
" habited by men of a different religion,
" would prevent my receiving any fuftenance
" without breaking thofe rules, which I have
" hitherto religioufly obferved. I therefore
" humbly requeft, that I may be permitted
" to refide, under as ftrict a guard as may be
" judged requifite, in fome place where thefe
" objections may be obviated."

- After a long and careful examination
made by the Board into the truth of this reprefentation, I moved*, " That the Sheriff
" and his Deputy fhould be directed to wait
" on the Chief Juftice, on the part of the
" Board, to reprefent to him the fituation of
" the Rajah Nundcomar, whofe religion, as
" he had informed the Board, had obliged
" him to deny himfelf fuftenance in the par-
" ticular circumftances of his prefent con-

* Page 557.

" finement;

" finement; and to defire the Chief Juftice
" would confider of granting the Prifoner
" fuch relief, as might be confiftent with the
" ftrict fecurity of his perfon to anfwer to the
" charges brought againft him; and that a
" copy of the latter part of the Rajah's Pe-
_"tion to the Board fhould be delivered to the
" Sheriff." Colonel Monfon and General
Clavering agreed.

The Governor General faid, " I object to
" the Motion, becaufe the fame reprefenta-
" tion may be made by the Prifoner himfelf
" to the Chief Juftice; and I think, therefore,
" it would be improper that it fhould be con-
" veyed to him through the authority of Go-
" vernment."

In reply to this meffage Sir Elijah Impey,
in his letter of the 9th of May, thought proper to fay *,

" I muft make it my requeft, that the
" Maha Rajah may be acquainted by the
" Board that, if he has any further appli-
" cation to make for relief, he muft ad-
" drefs himfelf immediately to the Judges,
" who will give all due attention to his re-
" prefentations; for fhould he continue to
" addrefs himfelf to the Board, that which

* Page 562.

" will,

" will, and can only be obtained from prin-
" ciples of juftice, may have the appearance
" of being obtained by the means of influence
" and authority, the peculiar turn of mind of
" the natives being to expect every thing from
" power, and little from juftice."

In another letter, dated May 15, 1775, he
fays * :

" I did not, nor do not queftion the autho-
" rity of the Board in receiving Petitions; I
" carefully reftricted what I faid *to this indivi-*
" *dual Prifoner*; I did not defire his Petitions
" fhould not be received; but, when received,
" if they were to require any thing from the
" Judges or the Court, that the anfwers given
" to thofe Petitions fhould be, that he muft
" apply himfelf directly to the Judges; and
" this I did to avoid the imputation I then
" alluded to, and which would be equally de-
" rogatory to the character of the Council,
" as that of the Judges.

" The particular reafon, which called upon
" me in this cafe, to make that requifition,
" was the reports publicly circulated in this
" town, that, if the Judges could not be pre-

* Page 564.

" vailed

" vailed upon to releafe the Maha Rajah, he
" he would be delivered by force."

This fuppofed report of an intention in the
Commander in Chief and two of the Council,
to releafe the Prifoner *manu forti,* was not in-
confiderately advanced or abandoned by the
learned Gentleman. After we had forced him
to declare, as he did in his letter to the Board
of the 30th of May 1775 *, " That he knew
" it to be totally groundlefs; that he again
" and again difclaimed ever having given
" any credit, and detefted the thought of
" adding weight to fo fcandalous a report,"
he revived it in his letter to the Secretary of
State, of the 20th of January 1776, in the following words: " It fhould be known that
" the conduct of the Council, *(meaning the*
" *majority)* to the Judges, and to the Pri-
" foner during his confinement, had raifed an
" almoft univerfal belief in the Natives, and
" even among the Europeans, that the Pri-
" foner would be *protected from juftice,* in de-
" fiance of the Court."—And now he re-
fumes, and infifts upon it once more at the Bar
of this Houfe. I leave it to him to reconcile an imputation of fuch a nature, if he can,
to that high approbation, with which he fays

* Page 569.

we

we afterwards received the execution of Nundcomar. But, in what light did General Clavering confider it ? Sir, the imputation of a
defign to refift the Civil Power, to oppofe the
Execution of Juftice, appeared to him not
only fo fcandalous, but fo dangerous, fo particularly levelled at *him*, as a Military Man,
as Commander in Chief of the Army, that
he thought it neceffary, for his fafety, to ex-
culpate himfelf from it by oath *. I fay, *for
his fafety*, becaufe I am firmly of opinion, that
he would have been in as great danger as Nundcomar, if the Judges could have found any
thing criminal to have laid to his charge.
Colonel Monfon and I, though not the immediate objects of that infamous calumny,
thought it right to take the fame oath. From
this extraordinary fact, I leave it to you to
conclude, what muft have been our opinion
of the perfonal fecurity of our fituation.

On the 30th of May, the Chief Juftice
thought fit to write us a very long letter (on
the fubject of our interpofition in behalf of
Nundcomar,) in which he faid ‡,

* Page 565.　　‡ Page 569.

H .　　　　　　" As

" As to communicating Petitions to the
" the Judges, I apprehend that no Board,
" even of the higheſt authority in England,
" can refer any matter, either to a Court of
" Juſtice, or any Judge thereof, otherwiſe
" than by ſuit legally inſtituted ."

On the 23d of June*, the Chief Juſtice declared from the Bench, that the Governor General and Council, whom he conſidered as nothing more than as Agents of the Eaſt India Company, could only apply to the Court by humble Petition, and that the Court could not receive in future any letters or meſſages but in that form.

Extract of a Declaration from the Bench, made by Sir ELIJAH IMPEY *on the 23d of June,* 1785.

" The Company, as well as all other Ap-
" pellants, muſt not claim it, but prefer an
" humble Petition. This being thus explain-
" ed, to prevent any further altercations of
" this nature, the Court muſt inform the
" Board that they cannot (reſpect being had

* Page 616.

" to

" to the dignity of his Majefty's Courts, and
" to the welfare of the country) receive in
" future any letter or meffages but in that
" form."

On the 27th of June *, we tranfmitted to
the Judges a tranflation of a letter addreffed
to the Governor General and Council, in favour of Nundcomar, by the Nabob Mobaric
ul Dowlah, Subadar of the Provinces of Bengal, Bahar, and Orixa; titular indeed, for to
that ftate was he reduced, but the only right-
ful reprefentative of the Sovereignty, and ftill
acknowledged to be the Nazim, or Chief
Criminal Magiftrate of the country. Whether the Judges gave any anfwer to that fpecific application from the Nabob, through the
Governor General and Council, I cannot difcover. I rather fufpect that, as Sir Elijah
Impey knew the reference had paffed *unanimoufly* at the Board, he thought it beft to
take no notice of what he could not conve-
niently condemn without a cenfure of his
friends.—But obferve how he acted, when he
found us alone. On the 20th of June, the

* Page 583.

H 2   Governor

Governor General and Council had refolved to
addreis the Judges in behalf of the Nabob's
Vakeel, for whom we claimed, as well on the
part of the Prince whom he reprefented, as on
the part of our Government, by whom he was
received, the rights and privileges of a public
Minifter *. Mr. Haftings and Mr. Barwell
diffented, and refufed to fign the letter. I
beg leave to read to you an extract from the
anfwer, which the Judges fent us the next
day by a Mafter in Chancery †:

" That the Court is of opinion, that all
" claims of individuals ought to be made di-
" rectly to the Court by the individuals, and
" not by the authority of the Governor Ge-
" neral and Council.

" That it is contrary to the principles of
" the Englifh Conftitution, for any perfon or
" perfons to addrefs a Court of Juftice by
" letter miffive, concerning any matter pend-
" ing before fuch Court ; and that the higher
" the ftation of the perfon or perfons fo ad-
" drefsing, the act is the more unconftitu-
" tional."

* Page 606—7.   † Page 610.

Finally,

Finally Sir, I beg leave to read to you an extract of what is called * *the unanimous opinion of the Court, delivered (on the 1st of July) by the Chief Justice, in consequence of a letter signed J. Clavering ;—George Monson ;—P. Francis.*

" It is with the deepest concern we find the
" Council still persist to address the Court by
" letter, on subjects pending in Court, or on
" which the Court have given their opinion ;
" and that, notwithstanding the frequent de-
" clarations, and unanimous opinion of the
" Court, upon the impropriety of that mode
" of address."

After all this had passed, it is not much to be wondered at, that General Clavering should resolve not to make any more applications in favour of Nundcomar.

You have seen, that we interceded for him with the Judges. You have seen, in what manner our intercession was received. It is proper you should know, what the subject and occasion were, which drew down so many censures and menaces upon us. As soon as we received Nundcomar's petition of the 8th of May, the conclusion and prayer of which

* Page 663.

we

we immediately refolved to communicate to
Sir Elijah Impey; we examined the Sheriff
and Under Sheriff, concerning the circumftances of Nundcomar's confinement, and of his
fituation in the goal. From their evidence it
appeared, that he was committed on the 6th;
and from that time, I think about forty
hours, had refufed to take any fuftenance.
The next day, the Chief Juftice's anfwer to
our meffage was received in Council.

He defired the Sheriff and Under Sheriff
to inform us " that Rajah Nundcomar was
" not committed by him, and that he had no
" authority to interfere in the affair, there be-
" ing felony exprefsly charged in the war-
" rant." General Clavering then faid*, " I
" acquaint the Board that I have received a
" letter from Mr. Jofeph Fowke, who is juft
" come from vifiting Maha Raja Nundcomar;
" acquainting me, that it is the opinion of
" the people, who were about him, that they
" do not think he can live another day with-
" out drink. He fays his tongue is much
" parched, but that his fpirit is firm. In the

* Page 560.

" converfation

" converfation that he had with the Raja, the
" Raja told him, *do not trouble yourfelf about
" me. The will of heaven muft be complied with.
" I am innocent.*" I immediately moved that
the goaler might be fent for to inform us whether Rajah Nundcomar had really taken no
fuftenance fince his confinement, and in what
fituation the Raja then was. When he came,
I queftioned him myfelf, and it appeared by
his examination, that the Rajah had then taken no fuftenance for fixty-three hours;—that
the jail was crowded; that it had not been fo
full before, and that there were at that time
twenty-three felons in it, befides other prifo-
ners. I then moved " that the information
" laid before the Board by General Clavering,
" and the further account given by the jailer,
" fhould be communicated to the Chief Juftice,
" by the Secretary, on the part of the Board;
" and that the Secretary fhould wait upon him
" accordingly as foon as the Board broke up."
This was agreed to and ordered.

On the fame day, we received a letter from
Sir Elijah Impey to inform us that he had
fent for the pundits, and examined them concerning the pretended fcruples of Nundcomar.
The refult was, *that there were no grounds for*

2 *altering*

altering the mode of confinement of the Maha Raja.
He affured us*, " that the Judges would,
" as far as by law they might, remit the ri-
" gour of the Englifh law, in all cafes,
" where its effects might be prejudicial to the
" natives on account of their religion; and
" perhaps in fome cafes, would yield even to
" prejudices, if national and deep rooted.
" But they muft not fuffer the pretence of
" religion to be fet up for the purpofes of
" eluding the ordinary courfe of the law."
Accordingly the unfortunate man was abandoned to his fate; or, if you will, to the unavoidable confequence of his own obftinacy.
Whether his fcruples were well, or ill founded,
is more than I am able to explain. We know
with certainty that the Gentoo religion is, in
a great degree, ceremonial ; and in a very low
degree, if at all, dogmatical. It prefcribes
many things to be performed, many others to
be abftained from, but not much to be believed. It forms the occupation, rather than the
creed of a mild, inoffenfive, innocent people.
To preferve what they think a religious purity,
to fave themfelves from what they deem to be

* Page 561.

indelible

indelible pollution; I do not fay that they
will act with vigour, (that perhaps is not in
their nature) but I know they will fuffer and
endure with a patience more than human.
Can you doubt that Nundcomar was in earneft
in the fcruples he profeft, when I tell you that,
while the Judges ~~were debating with us, whe-~~
~~ther he ought to be relieved or not~~, and while
Sir Elijah Impey debated the point with us,
whether Nundcomar ought to be relieved or
not, and while he was amufing himfelf with
writing us long letters on the fubject, the old
man, above feventy years of age, refolutely
perfifted in refufing all manner of food for
more than eighty hours ? In fo much that the
Judges themfelves, alarmed at the idea and
poffible confequences of an *illegal murder*, gave
an indirect permiffion to the jailor, as it were
without their knowledge, to pitch a tent for
Nundcomar out of the limits of the prifon, in
which, at proper hours, he might perform
his ablutions and prepare his food. Sir Elijah Impey takes care to tell you, what fpe-
cial pains he took to inform himfelf, whether there was any real foundation for the religious difficulties pretended by Nundcomar*.

* Page 561.

I   He

He sent the pundits, whom he calls *the keep-*
ers of the consciences and the oracles of the Gentoos,
to examine the place of his confinement, and
they, it seems, told him that *, " a Bramin
" could not properly perform his ablutions, or
" eat and drink in the place where Raja Nund-
" comar was confined. But, if he did, he
" would not lose his cast, but he must perform
" a penlance."

Now, Sir, it is proper you should know,
that these pundits, in point of circumstances
and situation, were very low and indigent per-
sons; that they received small salaries for
their attendance on the Supreme Court, and
were removeable at the pleasure of the Judges.
Admitting nevertheless that, in this state of
dependance, they might have had courage
enough to deliver an opinion adverse to the apparent inclination of the Chief Justice, on
whom they depended, and that the opinion,
which they did deliver, was sincere, it ought
not to have prevailed with Sir Elijah Impey
against what he saw was the internal conviction
of Nundcomar, demonstrated by a determina-
tion to die, rather than save his life by sub-
mitting to pollution. He ought to have

* Page 562.

known,

known, that the Hindoos are not only divided
into cafts, but that, in the fame caft, there
are different orders and degrees, not only diftinct in point of rank, but feparated by religious rules and inftitutions, attached and appro-
priated to every divifion of every caft, and
which can neither be renounced or invaded
without a crime. The Bramin of a lower clafs
is no judge even of the ceremonies, much lefs
of the religious fcruples of a fuperior Bramin.
When Nundcomar was informed of the report
made by the pundits, the old man fmiled, and
faid, " thefe men are not of *my* level. They
" are no judges of *my* confcience."

Want of food was not the only diftrefs, to
which this unfortunate man was obliged to
fubmit. He was confined in a miferable jail,
crowded with debtors and felons of all nations,
ranks and religions ; and though he might
have had every accommodation, which fuch a
place could afford, ftill I affirm, that it muft
have been to *him* not only a loathfome, but
a dangerous, cruel, and tyrannical confinement. Mr. Naylor, the Company's Attorney, committed by Sir Elijah Impey for a
contempt of the Court, in not anfwering interrogatories, died in confequence of being fhut

up

up there a few weeks. Others, to *my* knowledge, have fuffered by it feverely.

In fuch a prifon, we knew that Nundcomar
was perifhing for want of food.—That we felt
the moft ferious anxiety for his fituation, Sir
Elijah Impey may affect to doubt, if he thinks
proper. That General Clavering fent conftantly to enquire about his health, is charged
and admitted. But, in this offence, he had
accomplices, it feems, whom Sir Elijah Impey has thought it perfectly proper and becoming in him to include in the charge. For
the fake of calumniating the memory of Sir
John Clavering, he brings *the ladies of his
family* into public notice, into the judicial view
of the Houfe of Commons. Sir John Clavering's daughters are accufed of fending every
day to the prifon with compliments to the
Rajah, and inquiries about his health. One
would think that, even if there had been any
thing improper in what they did, the confideration due to their fex and youth, to their
beauty and accomplifhments, might have protected them from fo ungenerous an allufion to
their names and conduct. But it is in the ex-
ercife of their charity, in the difplay of that
benevolent virtue, which gives new luftre to
                                              youth

youth and beauty;—it is in the performance of the most amiable of all human duties, that the daughters of General Clavering are introduced to be evidence against their father, and even Lady Clavering against her husband. The charge means nothing, if it be not intended to convey, that General Clavering had some improper connection and correspondence with the accuser of Mr. Hastings. Without that application, the mention of the ladies of his family would be mere malice, and nothing else. But, why not accuse *me* too of the same offence? I was at least as guilty of it as they. I sent messages every day to Nundcomar. If, knowing his situation so exactly as I did from the Sheriff, I had neglected him at such a time, I must have lost all sense of humanity. For the same sort of purpose, we are accused of having paid a visit of ceremony to Rajah Nundcomar. I answer it by asking, *why should we not?* He was a person of the first rank in his own country.—He belonged to the highest order of the Bramins.—I believe he was their Chief.—He had been Prime Minister of the Government under Meer Jaffier, and his son. Was such a man not intitled to a visit from General Clavering, Colonel Monson and

me?—

me ?—In point of rank, he was far fuperior to
any of us. But, what was the fact ?—On the
day*, after he was examined before the
Judges, at Sir Elijah Impey's houfe, on a
charge of a pretended confpiracy againft Mr.
Haftings, when the charge was difmiffed, and
when his accufers were not even bound over to
profecute, we paid him a fhort vifit at his
houfe. I am fure it did not exceed ten minutes.
We faw plainly enough for what reafon he was
perfecuted, and we thought it became us to
pay him that compliment, as a public mark of
countenance and good opinion. We did not
promife him protection, for unfortunately we
had no power to protect him.

I have given you now an exact and faithful
account of a tranfaction, which, I think, Sir
Elijah Impey would never have appealed to, if
he had not been blinded by a guilty mind. He
flattered himfelf that he had contrived to make
it impoffible to detect the falfehood of his ftory.
I believe you are fatisfied, that he was, from the
firft, united in clofe collufion with Mr. Haftings;
that we were not miftaken in fufpecting, that
our fecret debates in Council were betrayed to

* 20th April, 1775.

him;—

him;—that our ordering Nundcomar's petition
to be burned, was founded on an apprehenfion
materially connected with that fufpicion;—
that, by that refolution, we never meant to
pronounce upon the fubftance or merits of the
petition; and that the learned gentleman himfelf never once thought of giving the conftruction to what we faid; or of drawing the conclufion from what we did, which he now advances, for the firft time, almoft thirteen
years after the event. If, on this laft material
point, there be yet a doubt in the mind of any
man, I can remove it by the beft of all evidence,
by that at leaft, which ufually makes the deep-
eft impreffion,—by the evidence of the party
againft himfelf. Sir Elijah Impey's letter to
the Secretary of State, dated the 20th of Jan-
nary 1776, is now before me. It confifts of
feventeen folio pages in print. It appears to
have been written on purpofe to vindicate his
character from the afperfions *uniformly* thrown
upon it, by Clavering, Monfon, and Francis,
for his conduct in the bufinefs of Nundcomar,
to charge them with having *conftantly* imputed
to the Court the moft atrocious motives for their
conduct, by ftrong infinuation, malignant far-
cafm, and fevere cenfure; and to accufe them
of attempting, on fundry occafions, to over-
awe,

awe, or reduce the authority of the Supreme Court.

I beg leave to read to you a few fhort paf-fages out of this ftudied performance*.

1. " The Governor General has within
" thefe few days communicated to me feveral
" Minutes, figned by General Clavering, Co-
" lonel Monfon, and Mr, Francis. They
" are feverally fraught with direct charges,
" or plain infinuations, againft the characters
" of the Judges, and the conduct of the
" Court of Judicature. Some feem more par-
" ticularly levelled at *me*.

2. " The crimes either directly charged up-
" on the Judges, or indirectly infinuated,
" (which, I think, we have more reafon to com-
" plain of, as being lefs liberal) are of fo hor-
" rid and deteftable a nature that, if they are
" well grounded, ought to fubject each of
" them to the higheft punifhment a Parlia-
" ment Impeachment can inflict, and brand
" their names with infamy to the lateft pof-
" terity.

3. " I do fincerely attribute the offenfive
" parts of the paragraphs to imaginations heat-
" ed by party difputes; and entertain fo high

* Vide Appendix to the firft Report of the Select Committee in 1781 ; No. 27.

" a fenfe

" a fenfe of the honour of the Gentlemen,
" that at a period fome diftance from the
" events, which fhall have given time for
" their judgements to cool, they *will* them-
" felves be fhocked at what they have wrote,
" and be willing to retract the charges."

I agree with this learned gentleman intire-
ly in the definition he has given of his crimes,
as well as in his opinion of the punifhment they
deferve. But I call upon him to explain to
you, if he can, why, in January 1766, he
looked forward to a *future* period for a *future*
retractation of the charges we had ftated, of
the falfehoods we had written againft him, if
it be true, as he now tells you, that we had
already abandoned thofe charges, if we had
already acknowledged the falfehood of our
affertions, and borne a clear unqueftionable
teftimony to the rectitude of his conduct.
The diftinction he endeavours to fet up between our *Minutes*, which he affirms he never
faw, and our public act in burning the paper,
will be no relief to him. He fays he never faw
our Minutes on the fubject. Be it fo, the affertion is incredible;—but I abandon that
queftion. At the prefent moment, I do not
defire you to believe what he denies, but only

K   to

to remember, what he has admitted. He was in poffeffion of the paper, and knew that we had ordered it to be deftroyed. If he had really conceived that, by that refolution, we meant to exprefs or imply an opinion of the *falfehood* of the contents, he ought to have concluded from it then, as he pretends to do now, that we ourfelves had acquitted him, by a public voluntary act of our own, of all the atrocious charges we had brought againft him. In that fenfe, if the act in queftion was any proof at all, it was full as good a proof of our favourable opinion of him, as any thing we could have faid in our Minutes upon the fubject.—In this long letter he never mentions or alludes to either one or the other. Yet that was the time, if ever, for him to have availed himfelf of the evidence of the perfons he calls his enemies, againft themfelves, and to invalidate any declarations they might have made againft him on other occafions : inftead of appealing then to the recorded fact,—to what he now calls irrefiftible evidence of our opinion in his favour, he exprefsly looks forward to a diftant day, when he expects that we fhall be ready to condemn ourfelves, when we fhall

be

be fhocked at what we have written, and be
willing to retract our charges.

4. " A public notification is profeffedly
" made to the Englifh nation, by which it is
" attempted to perfuade them, that the Court
" of Judicature, eftablifhed by his Majefty for
" protecting the natives of this country, and
" the Eaft India Company, from the violence
" and oppreffion of the Company's fervants,
" has been by the Judges converted into an
" execrable inftrument in the hands of Mr.
" Haftings, of deftroying the innocent native,
" for the fake of protecting the guilty fervants
" of the Company.

5. " It fhould be known, that the conduct
" of the Council to the Judges, and to the
" Prifoner during his confinement, had raifed
" an almoft univerfal belief in the natives,
" and even among the Europeans, that the
" prifoner would be *protected* from Juftice, in
" defiance of the Court.

6. " Raja Gourdafs (fon of Nundcomar) has
" caufed it to be intimated to me, that he was
" very defirous to pay his refpects to me, but
" is pofitively enjoined (he muft mean *forbidden*)
" entering my houfe by members of the Coun-
" cil."

K 2

I have

I have no recollection of this fact, nor do I believe one word of it. It is *possible*, I confess, that Raja Gourdafs might have been *very desirous to pay his respects to Sir Elijah Impey*, and for reafons perfectly coercive on the timid mind of a Hindoo. But he had no occafion for our confent. If he had afked me for my approbation of fuch a vifit, I fhould certainly have told him what I thought of it. The ftory in effect, which you are called upon to believe, is, that Raja Gourdafs was *bond-fide, very defirous to pay his respects to Sir Elijah Impey*; that is, to thank him for the murder of his father.

I fhall read but one fhort paragraph more out of this letter. To underftand it, you fhould know that, in one of our Minutes, we had faid, *we were ignorant of any attempts to over-awe or reduce the authority of the Supreme Court.*

" In anfwer to this, (Sir Elijah Impey fays)
" I muft refer to the letters fent me by the
" Council in May laft, concerning Nundco-
" mar; the letter addreffed to Mr. Juftice
" Hyde and Juftice Lemaiftre; the *univerfal*
" tenor of the Minutes of the Council, *whenever*
" the conduct of the Judges made part of their
" confultations.

In

In this paffage, the terms he has felected are
inclufive without exception. The *univerfal*
tenor of our Minutes was to attack, to condemn, and to reprobate the conduct of the Supreme Court. It was fo. I allow it. But,
when you have received that charge from Sir
Elijah Impey, when you have feen it deliberately ftated and infifted on by him,—in writing,—in a formal letter to the Secretary of
State for his Majefty's information, will you
permit him to tell you now, that it was not
true ?—will you fuffer him to aver againft his
own record ? will you endure to hear him fay,
that we did *not univerfally* condemn the Judges,
*whenever their conduct made part of our confulta-
tions?* for that on the very proceeding, which
was effentially in queftion, which, he fays,
we had charged as a crime, *that would brand
the names of the Judges with infamy to the lateft pof-
terity,* on this very proceeding, we had already
faid or done what muft have amounted in our
minds to a complete vindication of their conduct.—Even now, Sir, I am content to let
him choofe what fingle affertion he will abide
by.—But no man is at liberty to affert and deny
the truth of the fame propofition. You fee,
for what reafon Sir Elijah Impey was fo particular

cular in ſtating to the Committee, that he had never, till very lately, ſeen our Minutes of the 16th of Auguſt 1775.

Had he admitted that he had ſeen the Minutes in Calcutta, his letter to the Secretary of State would, upon his preſent ſhewing, have been a direct falſehood as a charge, and palpably defective as a defence. With thoſe Minutes before him, and underſtanding them in the ſenſe of approbation or even of acquittal, he could not have ſaid that we had *univerſally* condemned the conduct of the Supreme Court. Much leſs, while he was defending himſelf againſt the moſt atrocious imputations, particularly levelled at *him*, could he have omitted all mention of a fact ſo material to his defence, ſo irreſiſtible in its nature, as that we, who accuſed, had compleatly acquitted him.

I do not mean to give the Committee any farther trouble. Either the charge, which this learned Gentleman has brought againſt Sir John Clavering, Colonel Monſon and myſelf, is anſwered, or it is not in my power to anſwer it. Had he acted with the ſame candour to *me*, which my honourable friend has obſerved to *him* ;—had he thought proper to

deliver

deliver it in writing, I would have anfwered it in writing. Let him deliver it even now upon paper, and I pledge myfelf to anfwer it in the fame manner. Whether he does or no, it is my intention, though I do not abfolutely bind myfelf to do fo, to write down what I have faid, and to offer it to the Committee. Some way or other, I mean to put him in poffeffion of my defence. If his caufe be good, let him have all advantages in defending it. Let *him* go free while he accufes; and let *me* be bound down by my defence.

A word more, and I have done. Some fingular circumftances have contributed to mark me to the public eye as an object of attention. In our day it has happened, that two perfons, removed from ftations of the higheft truft, have been accufed of crimes the moft atrocious that ever yet were the fubject of accufation before any human tribunal;—one of them, on evidence which, in this Houfe at leaft I may prefume to fay, may be taken for conclufive. The other is only accufed.—The very firft thing thefe perfons think it neceffary to do, the very firft ftep they make towards their defence, is to declare that *I* am their enemy. Their conduct tells you, that I am

the

the firft difficulty, which they muft endeavcur to overcome ; that *I* am the fingle perfon, whom it is effential to their fafety to attack, to calumniate, to difqualify, to difcredit, and to remove. I am honoured by their objection. I am proud of the diftinction. In the bafe, vindictive meaning of enmity, I am not the perfonal enemy of either of them. But I defire it to be underftood, I wifh to have it proclaimed, wherever my name can be known, and to whatever period it fhall exift, that it is the poffeffion which I value nioft, that it is the inheritance which, above all others, I am anxious to tranfmit to my fon, that I am in moral principle oppofed to the principles of thefe men ; that I declare and avow immortal enmity to their minds and to their conduct, and that I truft that my character and principles will be known and diftinguifhed by an eternal oppofition and everlafting hoftility to the manners, the character, the conduct, and the hearts of Warren Haftings and Sir Elijah Impey.

APPENDIX.

APPENDIX.

No. I.

COPY *of a Petition from* Rajah Nundcomar, *confined in Goal, to the* Governor General *and* Council, *dated Calcutta, 8th May,* 1775 *:

Honourable Sir, and Sirs,

AFTER having been honoured with the confidence of the Nabob Jaffier Ally Khan, fo peculiarly the friend of the Englifh; after having difcharged the firft office in the Subah; after being now ten years retired from all public employments, and having feen my fon appointed to a diftinguifhed poft, with this teftimony, as I have been credibly informed, of the Governor's approbation of his father, that he inftated my fon in the poft, with a view to his profiting by my experience and wifdom, I might perhaps ftartle the Honourable Board with an addrefs from the

* Page 553.

L   common

common goal, had, I not in a degree prepared
them for fome fatal change in my fituation, by
a reprefentation I made in the month of
March, 1775, of the fevere menaces which
had been uttered againft me by the Governor
General. Where the firft magiftrate declares
his determined intention of hurting an individual to the utmoft of his power, the enemies
of the man fo marked for deftruction will
eagerly grafp at an opportunity of gratifying
their malice; the diffolute and abandoned
will find a fufficient inducement to perfecute
him from the hopes of gratifying the refentment of the man in power; and if the un-
happy man, fo devoted, have, by an upright
conduct, made the wicked his enemies, malice
and wickednefs may unite their endeavours to
complete his ruin. To advance a ftep further, fhould the firft man in the State countenance one * publicly known to be deftitute of
all moral principle, and as publicly known to
be the enemy of the perfon, againft whom he
has denounced his refentment : fhould he
treat a man of fuch principles with a degree
of diftinction far above his rank in life :

* Mohunperfaud.

fhould

should he admit him to private conferences
with him, what is the wretched object of his
refentment to expect? where shall he find an
afylum, when the whole body of the wicked
and abandoned is let loofe upon him?
I mean not now, however, to deprecate the
Governor General's refentment. The reafons
of the encouragement afforded to my enemies,
and the motives of the Governor General's
refentment againft me, will be fufficiently
explained to the world by the reprefentation I
have already made in a former addrefs to the
Honourable Board. Should my life be taken
away by the flagitious charge now laid againft
me, the facts before alluded to will remain
upon record, the witneffes will be ready, and
the proofs produceable, whenever the Governor
General has courage fufficient to hear them.
A charge which has been now thefe three
years depending in a Civil Court, without the
witneffes, upon whofe evidence I am committed, having been once produced or mentioned, has been laid againft me by men, who
are marked by the public as the moft turbulent
and abandoned. My only intention in fetting
forth the fervices I have done, and the character I have to an advanced age fupported,

L 2   is

is to introduce my requeft, that I might not fuffer upon fuch a charge, from the bafe accufation, a punifhment equal to that of death,—the violation of the moft facred duties of my religion. The Honourable Prefident, I am well affured, is fully fenfible of the facts I allude to. It may be requifite to explain to the reft of the Honourable Members of the Board, that the inftitutions of our religion ftrictly enjoin a number of ablutions, prayers, and other ceremonies to be performed by the Sect of Brahmins before they can take any kind of food. Nothing of this can be performed in the place where I now am; and could even thefe obftacles be furmounted, the place itfelf, as being inhabited by men of a different religion, would prevent my receiving any fuftenance, without breaking thofe rules, which I have hitherto religioufly obferved. I therefore humbly requeft that I may be permitted to refide, under as ftrict a guard as may be judged requifite, in fome place where thefe objections may be obviated.

(Signed)   NUNDCOMAR.

No. II.

No. II.

Fort William, 9th May, 1775 *.

COUNCIL.

The Jailer being arrived, is called before the Board, and asked his name : he answers, " Matthew Yandel."

Questions by Mr. Francis.

Q. Whether Rajah Nundcomar has refused to take any sustenance since his commitment; and whether you believe it to be true that he has received none ?

A. I do believe it to be true that he has received none. I am sometimes out upon business, but I don't know of his having received any.

Q. What situation is the Rajah now in with respect to his health, and his personal appearance ?

A. He appears to be very well, only a little daunted with the situation he is now in; —low in spirits.

Q. How many hours has the Rajah been in your custody ?

A. He

A. He came on Saturday night, a little after ten; it is now paſt one; ſo that he muſt have been at this time in confinement ſixty-three hours.

. *Governor General.—Q.* ·Have you any other priſoners of the Bramin caſt in the goal ?

A. I dare ſay I have, but I have not en-quired; we have generally of all caſts in the goal.

Mr. Francis.—Q. How many perſons have you in the goal, debtors and felons ?

A. Between ſixty and ſeventy perſons.

Q. Is it crowded.

A. Yes, fuller than in general; we have not had it ſo full before; we have about twenty-two or twenty-three felons; five or ſix uſed to be a great many. ·

No. III.

No. III.

Extract from the first Report from the Select Committee, in 1782 *.

The cafe of Mr. North Naylor, Attorney to the Company, is of itfelf fufficient to render all fuch complaints, in future, an affair of the extremeft hazard.

Mr. Naylor, who appears to have been a perfon of confiderable induftry and abilities, was employed by the Governor General and Council to defend that Board, and fome perfons of diftinction among the natives, againft the late fuits in the Supreme Court. The Supreme Court attached Mr. Naylor for a contempt, on account of fome fteps he had taken, under the direction, and in favour of his clients; and, on his refufal to anfwer a feries of interrogatories, (in which refufal he was fupported by his Clients) he was detained in the common goal at Calcutta, a miferable and peftilential place, upwards of a month. For thefe interrogatories, which your Committee conceive to be in many parts wholly unjuftifiable, they refer to their report of laft feffion, and to the Coffijurah Appendix to that report.

* Page 48.

(No. 23.)

(No. 23.) Mr. Naylor, who was in no good
ftate of health at the time of this rigorous
imprifonment, and having had during its
continuance, fome family misfortunes, died
foon after his releafe upon bail; his death
being in all probability, haftened, if not
caufed by his fufferings under confinement.

———————

No. IV.

Copy of a Note from Mr. Mackrabie, *Sheriff of
Calcutta, to Mr.* Francis, *dated* 11th May,
1775.

Raja Nundcomar has now a tent fixed on
the outfide of the prifon gate, for the purpofe of wafhing and eating. He has done
both this morning, but is not yet returned
into his apartments in the jail, fo that I cannot be admitted to him. Nilmony * has feen
him, and finds him fomewhat better, though
very weak. Laft night he was fo much al-

* Mr. Francis's Sircar, a Bramin.

tered,

tered, that I really thought him almoft in ex-
tremities—fo did Tolfrey. Upon a late reprefentation to the Judges, fome time after the application made by me, they gave directions
for his having this indulgence. It is, I find,
to appear as the fole act of the Jailor, to avoid
precedents. The authority was not given to
me ; and, upon my return to town, at mid-
night, I found the Raja informed, and orders
given for all the different preparations. You
fee how little fhare I have in it. I think
I fhould not be quoted ; I will give you fome
reafons, with the particulars at large, at
dinner,

I am ever faithfully,

Yours,

Thurfday Noon.   A. M.

M   No. V.

No. V.

Copy of a Letter from Mubbaric O'Dowlah, *Subahdar of Bengal, to the* Governor General *and* Council, *received* 27*th* June, 1775 *.

If feveral tranfactions of former times are to be tried by the Act lately tranfmitted from the King of Great Britain, it will occafion trouble and ruin to the inhabitants of this country. The affair of Maha Rajah Nundcomar, which is now before the Court, is really hard and rigorous ; for, fhould the crime of which he is accufed, be proved againft him in the faid Court, the cuftom of this country does not make it deferving of capital punifhment : nor, as I am informed, was life formerly forfeited for it in your country; that has only been common for a few years paft. The Maha Rajah has tranfacted affairs of the greateft importance. When Meer Coffim Ally Khan had taken the refolution to ruin and expel the Englifh, the Maha Rajah, in particular, exerted himfelf to the utmoft, with my father, in fupplying them with grain and money for the ufe

* Page 583.

of

of their troops. The fervices of the Mahá Rajah on this occafion are well known to the King of Hindoftan; certainly he never could have committed fo contemptible a crime. People employed in important affairs will undoubtedly have many enemies; and thofe, who have been active in the affair of Nundcomar, have long been his declared foes. Taking therefore into confideration the welfare of the people, I beg in particular, with refpect to this affair, that the Rajah's execution may be fufpended till the pleafure of his Majefty, the King of England, fhall be known.

RESOLVED,

That a Copy of this tranflation be tranfmitted with the following Letter to the Chief Juftice and Judges of the Supreme Court of Judicature.

To Sir Elijah Impey, *Chief Juftice*, Robert Chambers, S. C. Lemaiftre, *and* J. Hyde, *Judges of the Supreme Court of Judicature.*

GENTLEMEN,

We have this inftant received a letter from his Excellency, the Nabob Mubbarick O'Dowlah, Muttuwanum ul Mulluk, Ferofe Jung Bahader, through the hands of Roy

Rada

Rada Churn, his public Vakeel, containing an interceffion in behalf of Maha Rajah Nundcomar; we conceive it to be regular in this Board to tranfmit it to you, and of which we fhall inform the Nabob.

We are, &c.

(Signed) WARREN HASTINGS,
          J. CLAVERING,
          GEO. MONSON,
Fort William,   RICH. BARWELL,
27th June, 1775. P. FRANCIS.

No. VI.

Extract of Secret Confultations. Fort *William* *May* 16th 1775*.

General Clavering. " I requeft the favour of
" the Governor General that he, as one of his
" Majefty's Juftices of the Peace, will be
" pleafed to receive my affidavit, that either
" in my corporate capacity as a Member of the

* Page 565.

" Board

" Board, or as an individual, I never conceiv-
" ed any intention, nor ever heard of such
" an intention, suggested to me by any body,
" that the Maha Rajah Nundcomar was to be
" delivered by force from the confinement he
" is in. I think it neceſſary to make this affi-
" davit, becauſe I find in a letter, addreſſed
" to the Governor General and Council, by
" Sir Elijah Impey, the Chief Juſtice of the
" Supreme Court of Judicature, a paragraph,
" in which he mentions, that he, the Chief
" Juſtice, was induced, contrary to his belief,
" to make the application to the Board upon
" the 9th inſtant, that the Governor General
" and Council ſhould acquaint Maha Rajah
" Nundcomar to apply directly to the Judges
' inſtead of his applying to them, as there were
" reports, publicly circulated in the town,
" that, if the Judges could not be prevailed
" upon to releaſe Maha Rajah Nundcomar,
" he would be delivered by force; and fur-
" ther I deſire to declare, that I never heard
" of ſuch a report till I read it in Sir Elijah
" Impey's letter."

Governor General. " I beg leave to ſubmit
" it to the conſideration of the General, whe-
" ther, on a reviewal of the words, made uſe
                                        " of

" of by the Chief Juftice in his letter, there is
" a neceffity for his giving a mere rumour fo
" much confequence, as to take and enter
" upon the public records a folemn oath for
" the refutation of it. I am morally certain,
" that neither the Chief Juftice, nor any other
" reafonable perfon could entertain the moft
" diftant fufpicion of an intention in the Gene-
" ral, or any other Member of this Board, to
" commit fo flagrant an outrage on the laws of
" their country, as to attempt to refcue by
" force a man committed to gaol under a legal
" authority.—I do not underftand the words of
" the Chief Juftice's letter as expreffing more
" than a mere popular opinion, which is often
" known to prevail without foundation, and
" however improbable, to operate to the pro-
" duction of the worft confequences. I have
" heard of many reports faid to be circulated by
" Nundcomar, or his dependants, but I have
" paid fo little attention to them, that I really
" cannot recollect any of the purport here al-
" luded to ; but do not think it neceffary my-
" felf to follow the General in the affidavit
" propofed to be taken by him, if he fhall
" ftill adhere to his firft declaration, for the
" refutation of a charge, which I think can
" nei-

" neither light upon myfelf, nor any other
" Member of the Council."

· *General Clavering.* " I conceive that a de-
" claration, fimilar to that which I have
" made, is abfolutely neceffary for the juftifica-
" tion of each Member of this Government;
" becaufe the report of an attempt to deliver
" by force the Maha Rajah is made the ground,
" which Sir Elijah Impey acquaints the Board
" he had for his application to us to direct
" Maha Rajah Nundcomar to apply for relief
" henceforward to the Judges, and not to the
" Council. By making this propofition, I
" do not conceive myfelf more implicated in
" the charge brought (as it feems to me)
" againft the Government, that any other
" Member of it; but in times, when people
" make a trade of informations, I think *no
" man can be fafe from the danger*, attending up-
" on them, efpecially when reports, which are
" credited by a Chief Juftice (notwithftanding
" his declaration to the contrary) might, in
" fuch fufpicious times, be eafily converted ·
" into a criminal accufation. It is for thefe
" reafons, that I defired that my own affidavit
" might be taken, and I could wifh that the
  " fame .

" fame folemnity might be obferved by every
" Member of the Board."

Colonel Monfon. " From the letter of Sir
" Elijah Impey now before the Board, in
" which there are infinuations, which may
" poffibly be interpreted to my prejudice and
" difadvantage, I requeft that my affidavit
" may be taken, that I never had an intention
" either in my public or private character, to
" ufe any force to releafe Maha Rajah Nund-
" comar from his confinement by the Juftices
" of the Peace; nor did I ever hear, that fuch
" a rumour prevailed in the town of Calcutta,
" until I was informed of it by the Chief Juf-
" tice's letter."

Mr. Francis. " I beg leave to declare upon
" oath, that, until I faw the letter from Sir
" Elijah Impey, I never heard of the report
" mentioned therein; and that I do not be-
" lieve that an intention, to deliver the Maha
" Rajah Nundcomar by force from his con-
" finement, was ever thought of by any Mem-
" ber of this Board.

Fort William, May 16*th,* 1775.
" Whereas it has been afferted by Sir Eli-
" jah Impey, in a letter, written by him to
" the Governor General and Council, on the
" 15th

" 15th inftant, that reports had been publicly
" circulated in this town, that, if the Judges
" could not be prevailed upon to releafe the
" Maha Rajah Nundcomar, he would be de-
" livered by force; we hereby moft folemnly
" declare, that we never ourfelves conceived
" fuch an intention, nor ever heard of fuch a
" defign in any Member of the Government,
" or by any body elfe; nor did we ever hear
" mention of fuch a report, till we read it
" in Sir Elijah Impey's letter above-menti-
" oned."

  (Signed) " JOHN CLAVERING.
       " GEORGE MONSON.
       " PHILIP FRANCIS.

Sworn before me,
 (Signed) " WARREN HASTINGS."

 " *The Governor General* has declined giving
" in the affidavit, as deeming it unneceffary,
" but declares his entire conviction and affu-
" rance, that no Member of this Board ever
" conceived an intention of ufing force for the
" releafe of Maha Raja Nundcomar from his
" imprifonment."

 Governor General. " Having already de-
" clared that I thought it unneceffary to take

      N   " the

" the affidavit, which has been propofed, I
" fhall content myfelf with the declaration,
" contained in the preceding Minute, at the
" fame time deeming myfelf under the like
" obligation to adhere to the ftrict line of
" truth, in every declaration made by me
" upon record, as if I was under the tie of an
" oath."

No. VII.

Tranflation of Nundcomar's *Petition, which was
laid before the* Governor General *and* Council,
by Sir John Clavering, 14*th Auguft,* 1775;
and prefented to the Houfe of Commons *by*
Sir Elijah Impey, *on the 8th February,*
1788.

To the Governor General *and* Council.

Within thefe three Soubahs of Bengal,
Bahar, and Oriffa, the manner in which I
have lived, and the honor and credit which I
have poffeffed * : formerly the Nazims of all

* Something wanting here to compleat the fenfe.

thefo

thefe Souhabs afforded attention and aid to
my good name; and from the prefence of
the King of Hindoftan I received munfib of
five thoufand, and from the beginning of the
Company's adminiftration, in confideration of
my good wifhes to the King, the Gentlemen
who had the direction of affairs at this place,
and at this time the Governor, Mr. Haftings,
who is at the head of affairs, did hold, and do
hold me in refpect ; never did any lofs to the
State, or oppreffion of the Ryots proceed from
me : at this time, for the fault of reprefenting
a juft fact, which, for the intereft of the King,
and the relief of the people, I in a fmall degree made known, many Englifh gentlemen
have become my enemies; and having no
other means to conceal their own actions,
deeming my deftruction of the utmoft expe-
diency for themfelves, revived an old affair
of Mohun Perfaud, which had formerly been
repeatedly found to be falfe; and the Governor knowing Mohun Perfaud to be a notorious
liar, turned him out of his houfe, and themfelves becoming his aiders and abettors ; and
Lord Impey, and the other Judges have tried
me by the Englifh laws, which are contrary to
the cuftoms of this Country, in which there

was

was never any such administration of justice
before, and taking the evidence of my enemies in proof of my crime, have condemned
me to death :—But by my death the King's
justice will let the actions of no person remain
concealed. And now, that the hour of death
approaches, I shall not, for the sake of this
world, be regardless of the next, but repre-
sent the truth to the Gentlemen of the Council.
The forgery of the bond of which I am accused, never proceeded from me. Many prin-
cipal people of this country, who were acquainted with my honesty, frequently re-
quested of the Judges to suspend my execution till the King's pleasure should be known;
but this they refused, and unjustly take away
my life. For God's sake, Gentlemen of the
Council, you who are just, and whose words
are truth, let not me undergo this injury,
but wait for the King's pleasure. If I am unjustly put to death, I will, with my family,
demand justice in the next life. They put me
to death out of enmity and partiality to the
Gentlemen who have betrayed their trust; and
in this case, the thread of life being cut, I in
my last moment again request, that you,
Gentlemen, will write my case particularly to
the

the juſt King of England.—I ſuffer, but my innocence will certainly be made known to him.

————————

No. VIII.

The following is the relation of Mr. Mackraby, the Sheriff.

Hearing that ſome perſons had ſuppoſed Maha Raja Nundoomar would make an addreſs to the people at his execution, I have committed to writing the following Minutes of what paſſed both on that occaſion, and alſo upon my paying him a viſit in priſon the preceding evening, while both are freſh in my remembrance.

Friday evening, the 4th of Auguſt, upon my entering his apartment in the goal, he aroſe and ſaluted me in his uſual manner. After we were both ſeated, he ſpoke with great eaſe and ſuch uncommon unconcern, that I really doubted whether he was ſenſible of his approaching fate; I therefore bid the interpreter inform him that I was come to ſhew

him

him this laſt mark of reſpect, and to aſſure him
that every attention ſhould be given the next
morning which could afford him comfort on
ſo melancholy an occaſion ; that I was deeply
concerned that the duties of my office made
me of neceſſity a party in it, but that I would
attend to the laſt, to ſee that every deſire he
had ſhould be gratified ; that his own pallankeen and his own ſervants ſhould attend him,
and that ſuch of his friends, who I underſtood
were to be preſent, ſhould be protected. He
replied, that he was obliged to me for
this viſit, that he thanked me for all my
favours, and intreated me to continue it to his
family ; that fate was not to be reſiſted, and
put his finger to his forehead, " God's will
" muſt be done." He deſired I would preſent his reſpects and compliments to the
* General, Colonel Monſon, and Mr. Francis, and pray for their protection of † Rajah
Gourdaſs ; that they would pleaſe to look
upon him now as the head of the Bramins.
His compoſure was wonderful ; not a ſigh
eſcaped him, nor the ſmalleſt alteration of

* The General, Sir John Clavering.
† Rajah Gourdaſs, his ſon.

voice

voice or countenance, though I underftood
he had not many hours before taken a folemn
and affectonate leave of his fon-in-law Roy
Radichurn. I found myfelf fo much fecond
to him in firmnefs, that I could ftay no longer.
Going down ftairs, the jailor informed me,
that fince the departure of his friends, he had
been writing notes and looking at accounts in
his ufual way. I began now to apprehend
that he had taken his refolution, and fully
expected that he would be found dead in the
morning; but on Saturday the 5th, at feven,
I was informed that every thing was in readi-
nefs at the goal for the execution. I came
there about half an hour paft feven; the
howlings and lamentations of the poor
wretched people who were taking their laft
leave of him is not to be defcribed. I have
hardly recovered the firft fhock while I write
this, above three hours afterwards. As foon
as he heard I was arrived, he came down into
the yard, and joined me in the jailor's apartment. There was no lingering about him,
no affected delay; he came chearfully into
the room, made the ufual falam, but would
not fit till I took a chair near him. Seeing
fomebody, I forget who, look at a watch,
he

got up, and faid he was ready, and immediately turning to three Bramins, who were to
attend and take care of his body, he embraced
them all clofely, but without the leaft mark
of melancholy or depreffion on his part, while
they were in agonies of grief and defpair. I
then looked at my own watch, told him the
hour I had mentioned was not arrived, that it
wanted above a quarter of eight, but that I
fhould wait his own time, and that I would
not rife from my feat without a motion from
him. Upon its being recommended to him,
that, at the place of execution, he would give
fome fignal when he had done with this world,
he faid he would fpeak. We fat about a
quarter of an hour longer, during which he
addreffed himfelf more than once to me;
mentioned Rajah Gourdafs, the General, Colonel Monfon, and Mr. Francis, but without
any feeming anxiety; the reft of the time, I
believe he paffed in prayer; his lips and tongue
moving, and his beads hanging upon his hand.
He then looked to me and arofe, fpoke to fome
of the fervants of the goal, telling them that
any thing he might have omitted Rajah Gourdafs would take care of, then walked chearfully to the gate, and feated himfelf in his
pallan-

pallankeen, looking round him with perfect
unconcern. As the Deputy Sheriff and I
followed, we could make no obfervation upon
his deportment till we all arrived at the place
of execution. The croud there was very
great, but not the leaft appearance of a riot.
The Rajah fat in his pallankeen upon the
bearers' fhoulders, and looked around at firft
with fome attention. I did not obferve the
fmalleft difcompofure in his countenance or
manner, at fight of the gallows or any of the
ceremonies paffing about it. He afked for the
Bramins, who were not come up, and fhewed
fome earneftnefs, as if he apprehended the
execution might take place before their arrival.
I took that opportunity of affuring him, I
would wait his own time, " it was early in the
" day, and there was no hurry." The Bramins foon after appearing, I offered to remove
the officers, thinking that he might have
fomething to fay in private, but he made a
motion not to do it, and faid he had only a
few words to remind them, of what he had
faid concerning Rajah Gourdafs, and the care
of his * Zenana. He fpoke to me, and de-

* Zenana. Properly the apartments of the women;
meaning here, in the fenfe of a Bramin who does not admit of polygamy, his wife and children.

O   fired

fired that the men might be taken care of, as they were to take charge of his body, which he defired repeatedly might not be touched by any of the bye-ftanders; but he feemed not the leaft alarmed or difcompofed at the croud around him. There was fome delay in the neceffary preparations, and from the awkward-nefs of the people; but he was no way defirous of protracting the bufinefs, but repeatedly told me he was ready. Upon my afking him if he had any more friends he wifhed to fee, he anfwered he had many, but this was not a place, nor an occafion to look for them. " Did he apprehend there might be any pre- " fent, who could not get up for the crowd ?" He mentioned one, whofe name was called ; but he immediately faid, it was of no confe-quence, " probably he had not come." He then defired me to remember him to General Clavering, Colonel Monfon, and Mr. Francis, and looked with the greateft compofure. When he was not engaged in converfation, he lay back in his pallankeen, moving his lips and tongue as before. I then caufed him to be afked about the fignal he was to make, which could not be done by fpeaking, on ac-count of the noife of the croud. He faid he would make a motion with his hand; and,

when

when it was reprefented to him that it would be neceffary for his hands to be tied, in order to prevent any involuntary motion, and I recommended his making a motion with his feet, he faid he would. Nothing now remained, except the laft painful ceremony. I ordered his pallankeen to be brought clofe under the gallows, but he chofe to walk, which he did more erect than I have generally feen him. At the foot of the fteps, which lead to the ftage, he put his hands behind him to be tied with a handkerchief; looking round at the fame time, with the utmoft unconcern. Some difficulties arifing about the cloth, which fhould be tied over his face, he told the people that it muft not be done by one of us. I prefented to him a fubaltern feapoy officer, who is a Bramin, and came forward with his handkerchief in his hand, but the Rajah pointed to a fervant of his own, who was laying proftrate at his feet, and beckoned him to do it. He had fome weaknefs in his feet, which, added to the confinement of his hands, made him mount the fteps with difficulty, but he fhewed not the leaft reluctance, fcrambling rather forward to get up. He then ftood erect on the ftage, whilft I examined his countenance as

fted-

ftedfaftly as I could, till the cloth covered it, to fee if I could obferve the fmalleft fymptom of fear or alarm, but there was not a trace of it. My own fpirits funk, and I ftepped into my pallankeen; but before I was well feated, he had given the fignal, and the ftage was removed. I could obferve, when I was a little recovered, that his arms lay back in the fame pofition in which I faw them firft tied, nor could I perceive any contortion on that fide of his mouth and face which were vifible. In a word, his fteadinefs, compofure, and refolution throughout the whole of this melancholy tranfaction, were equal to any examples of fortitude I have ever read or heard of. The body was taken down, after hanging the ufual time, and delivered to the Bramins for burning.

F I N I S.

www.ingramcontent.com/pod-product-compliance
Lightning Source LLC
Chambersburg PA
CBHW031443280326
41927CB00038B/1578